My Pocket Guide

TEXAS

By Carole Marsh

D0790363

The GALLOPADE GANG

Carole Marsh
Bob Longmeyer
Michele Yother
Michael Marsh
Sherry Moss
Chad Beard
Sue Gentzke
Cecil Anderson
Steven Saint-Laurent
Deborah Sims
Andrew Brim
Andrea Detro
John Raines
Karin Petersen
Billie Walburn
Doug Boston
Kim Holst
Jennifer McGann
Ellen Miller
William Nesbitt, Jr.
Kathy Zimmer
Wanda Coats

Published by
GALLOPADE INTERNATIONAL

www.texasexperience.com
800-536-2GET • www.gallopade.com

©2000 Carole Marsh • First Edition • All Rights Reserved.
Character Illustrations by Lucyna A. M. Green.
No part of this publication may be reproduced in whole or in part, stored in a retrieval system, or transmitted in any form or by any means, electronic, mechanical, photocopying, recording or otherwise, without written permission from the publisher.

The Texas Experience logo is a trademark of Carole Marsh and Gallopade International, Inc. A free catalog of The Texas Experience Products is available by calling 800-536-2GET, or by visiting our website at www.texasexperience.com.

Gallopade is proud to be a member of these educational organizations and associations:

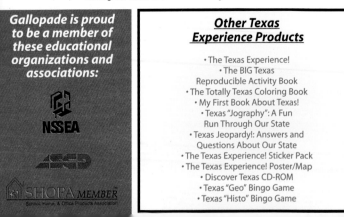

SHOPA MEMBER
School, Home, & Office Products Association

Other Texas Experience Products

• The Texas Experience!
• The BIG Texas Reproducible Activity Book
• The Totally Texas Coloring Book
• My First Book About Texas!
• Texas "Jography": A Fun Run Through Our State
• Texas Jeopardy!: Answers and Questions About Our State
• The Texas Experience! Sticker Pack
• The Texas Experience! Poster/Map
• Discover Texas CD-ROM
• Texas "Geo" Bingo Game
• Texas "Histo" Bingo Game

A Word From the Author... (okay, a few words)...

Hi!

Here's your own handy pocket guide about the great state of Texas! It really will fit in a pocket—I tested it. And it really will be useful when you want to know a fact you forgot, to bone up for a test, or when your teacher says, "I wonder . . ." and you have the answer—instantly! Wow, I'm impressed!

Get smart, have fun!

Carole Marsh

Texas Basics explores your state's symbols and their special meanings!

Texas Geography digs up the what's where in your state!

Texas History is like traveling through time to some of your state's great moments!

Texas People introduces you to famous personalities and your next-door neighbors!

Texas Places shows you where you might enjoy your next family vacation!

Texas Nature - no preservatives here, just what Mother Nature gave to Texas!

All the real fun stuff that we just HAD to save for its own section!

Who Named You?

Texas' official state name is…

Texas

Word Definition

OFFICIAL: appointed, authorized, or approved by a government or organization

Texas is one of the states to be on a year-2004 commemorative quarter! Look for it in cash registers everywhere!

Statehood: December 29, 1845

Texas was the ***28***th state to ratify the U.S. Constitution.

Coccinella Noemnotata is my name!

What A Great Name!

Texas was named for the Caddo Indian word, *Tejas*. Native Americans greeted the Europeans with "Tejas," which means friends or allies. Spanish explorers then adopted the word to mean both the people and the land. Eventually, Europeans changed the pronunciation of *Tejas*, and that's how we get Texas!

The Caddo were part of a confederacy of smaller groups of Native-Americans who preserved peace and order.

What's In A Name?

"Texas" is not the only name by which the state is recognized. Like many other states, Texas has other nicknames, official and unofficial!

State Nicknames

Lone Star State

Friendship State

Texas is called the Lone Star State because of the single star on the state flag, a reminder of its decade-long experience as a separate nation.
Wooow! You learn something new everyday!

State Capital:
Austin

During 1836, Washington-on-the-Brazos, Harrisburg, Galveston, Velasco, and Columbia served as temporary capitals before moving to Houston in 1837. Originally called Waterloo, Austin was renamed for the Father of Texas. A joint congressional commission first decided Austin should be Texas' capital in 1839.

Established: 1839

Originally Called: Waterloo

The Texas State Capitol building is 313 feet (95 meters) tall and is made of pink granite.

Word Definition

CAPITAL: a town or city that is the official seat of government
CAPITOL: the building in which the government officials meet

Who's in Charge Here?

Texas' has three branches:

GOVERNMENT

LEGISLATIVE | EXECUTIVE | JUDICIAL

The legislative branch is called the Texas Legislature.

LEGISLATIVE	EXECUTIVE	JUDICIAL
Two Houses: the Senate (31 members); House of Representatives (150 members)	A governor, lieutenant governor, and attorney general	Supreme Court & Court of Criminal Appeals nine justices each

The number of representatives is determined by population, which is counted in the census every ten years; the numbers above are certain to change as Texas grows and prospers!

When you are 18 and register according to Texas laws – you can vote! So please do! Your vote counts!

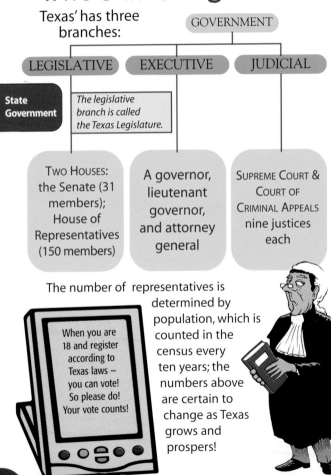

State Flag

The blue represents loyalty, the white represents strength or purity, and the red represents bravery or courage.

Our State Pledge: Honor the Texas Flag. I pledge allegiance to thee, Texas, one and indivisible.

Adopted January 25, 1839 when Texas was still a Republic, the Texas State flag is always found atop the state capitol, and all state, city and town buildings.

State Seal

The state seal has a five pointed star with a live oak branch and an olive branch.

MOTTO: a sentence, phrase, or word expressing the spirits or purpose of an organization or group

State Motto

Friendship

Texas' seal was adopted officially in 1992. The Texas State Seal has an obverse, the front, and a reverse, the back.

Adopted in 1930 from the meaning of the Caddo word, *Tejas*, meaning friends or allies.

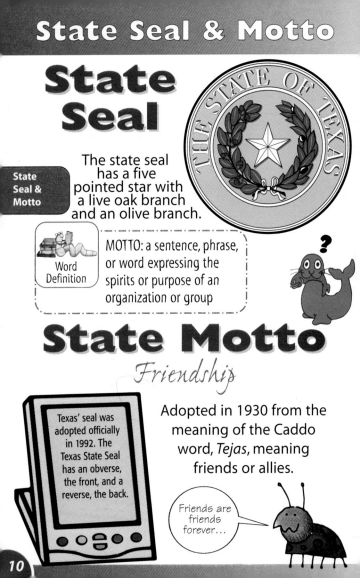

Birds of A Feather

The state bird of Texas is the Mockingbird *mimus polyglottos.* It copies the songs of other birds. Mockingbirds can also copy other sounds like a dinner bell.

Officially recognized in 1927, the Mockingbird became Texas' state bird at the request of the Texas Federation of Women's Clubs.

State Tree

Pecan

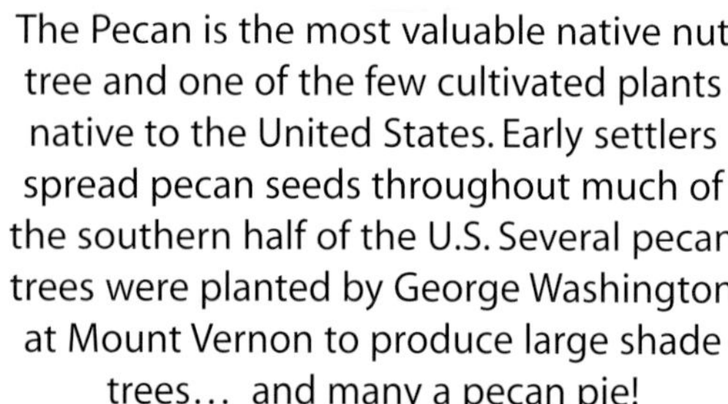

The Pecan is the most valuable native nut tree and one of the few cultivated plants native to the United States. Early settlers spread pecan seeds throughout much of the southern half of the U.S. Several pecan trees were planted by George Washington at Mount Vernon to produce large shade trees… and many a pecan pie!

Bluebonnet

The Bluebonnet became Texas' state flower in 1901, at the request of the Society of Colonial Dames in Texas. The flower is also called buffalo clover, wolf flower, and *el conejo* (the rabbit).

Prickly Pear Cactus

The Prickly Pear Cactus became Texas' state plant in 1995. Over 100 species of cacti are Texas residents. Ouch!

The suggestion by John Nance Garner that the cactus become Texas' state flower was rejected by the legislature in favor of the bluebonnet.

State Large Mammal

Texas Longhorn

State Large Mammal

Once thought to be a stringy animal, the Texas longhorns have been developed into higher quality stock, which live longer, have more calves, and don't get sick as often.

The Longhorn is also the mascot at the University of Texas. Students there are called "Longhorns." Hook 'em, Horns!

RIDDLE: If the state flower got mixed up with the Texas Longhorn, what would you have?

ANSWER: A Blue Horn... or a Long Bonnet?

Lightning Whelk

Lightning Whelks are found only on the Gulf Coast. A whelk is also known as a sea snail because of its spiral shell. Can you find one here?

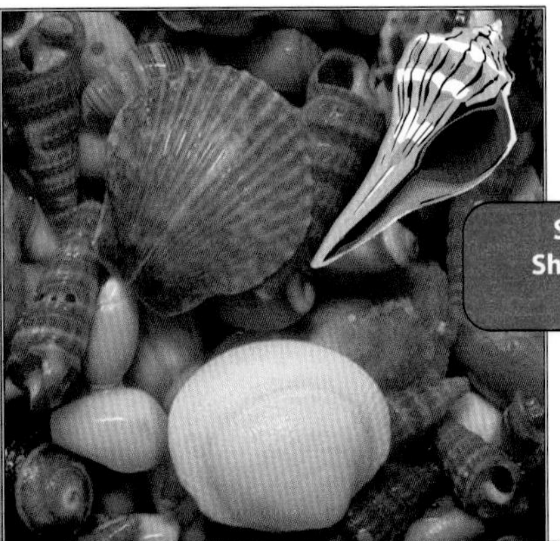

Whelks are meat eaters. Sometimes they eat oysters and other bivalves. They also eat dead fish and crabs.

Blue Topaz

Texas' state gem, the Blue Topaz, can be found in the Llano uplift area. It is especially beautiful in the Lone Star Cut.

Rodeo

The Rodeo was named the official state sport in 1997.

State Sport

Texas Cowboys invented the Rodeo. The first rodeo was held in Pecos, Texas in 1883. Rodeos include events like bulldogging, saddle bronc riding, and calf roping.

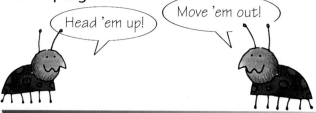

State Song

Texas, Our Texas

Words by Gladys Yoakum Wright and William J. Marsh, music by William J. Marsh. Adopted in 1929.

Texas, our Texas! All hail the mighty State!
Texas, our Texas! So wonderful, so great!
Boldest and grandest, withstanding every test;
O empire wide and glorious,
  you stand supremely blest.

God bless you, Texas! And keep you brave and strong,
That you may grow in power and worth,
  throughout the ages long.

Texas, O Texas! Your freeborn single star,
Sends out its radiance to nations near and far.
Emblem of freedom! It sets our hearts aglow,
With thoughts of San Jacinto and glorious Alamo.
Texas, dear Texas! From tyrant grip now free,
Shines forth in splendor your star of destiny!
Mother of Heroes! We come your children true,
Proclaiming our allegiance, our faith, our love for you.

REMEMBER THE ALAMO
TEXAS ONE AND INDIVISIBLE

The Square Dance

An American folk dance related to the English country dance and French ballroom dance. It includes squares, rounds, clogging, contra, line, the Virginia reel, and heritage dances.

In 1895, the Morning Star Hotel in Anson held a "Cowboy's Christmas Ball" which featured square dancing until dawn.

State Insect

The Monarch is found throughout the world but mainly in North America. Each fall, monarch butterflies migrate south to California, Florida, and Mexico. In the two-year lifetime of most of the butterflies, the monarch makes the trip twice.

Butterflies cannot fly if their body temperature is less than 86°F (30°C). At air temperatures below this, they must "warm up" their flight muscles by sunning their bodies or shivering their wings.

Guadalupe Bass

A member of the *Micropterus* family. It is one of a group of fish collectively known as black bass.

The Guadalupe bass was named the state fish in 1989.

Broiled Bass

Put a bass filet on foil. Drizzle with lemon juice. Sprinkle with salt and pepper. Add shredded smoked ham and broil fish until done.

A State in Good Shape

Texas forms a rough triangle along the southern border and has a thick area sticking up in the north called a panhandle.

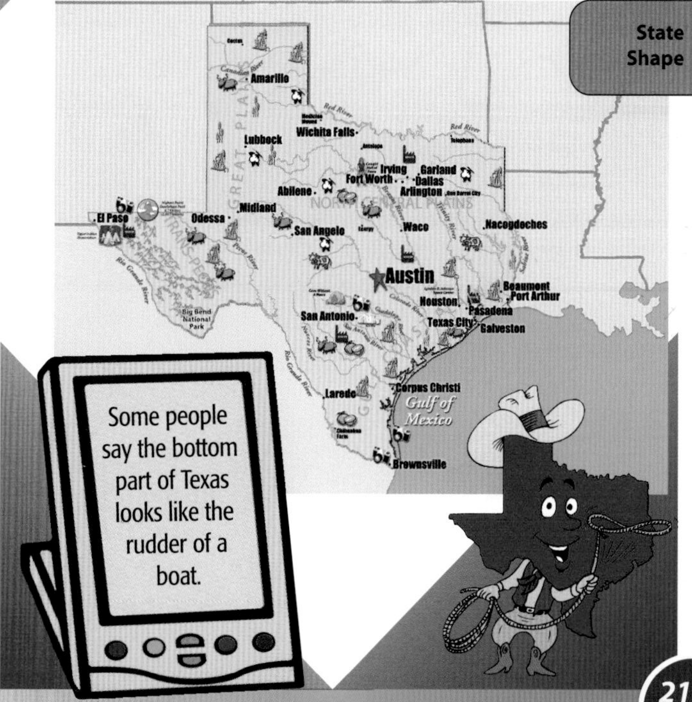

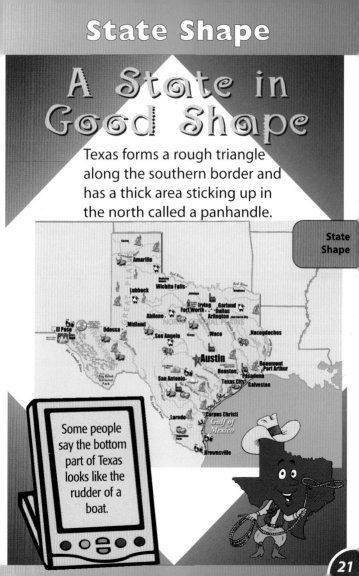

State Location

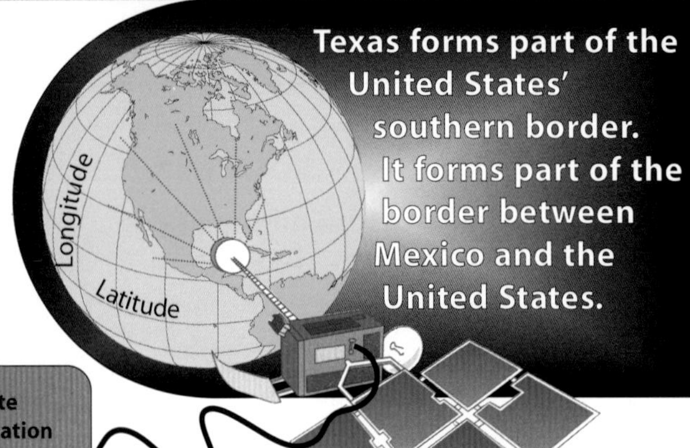

Texas forms part of the United States' southern border. It forms part of the border between Mexico and the United States.
Longitude
Latitude

State Location

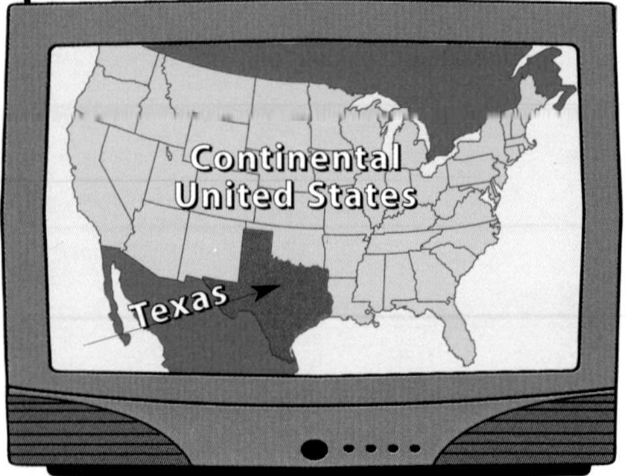

Continental United States
Texas

Word Definition

LATITUDE: Imaginary lines which run horizontally east and west around the globe
LONGITUDE: Imaginary lines which run vertically north and south around the globe.

These border Texas:

States: Oklahoma, Arkansas, Louisiana, New Mexico

Bodies of water: Gulf of Mexico, Red River, Rio Grande, Sabine River

Country: Mexico

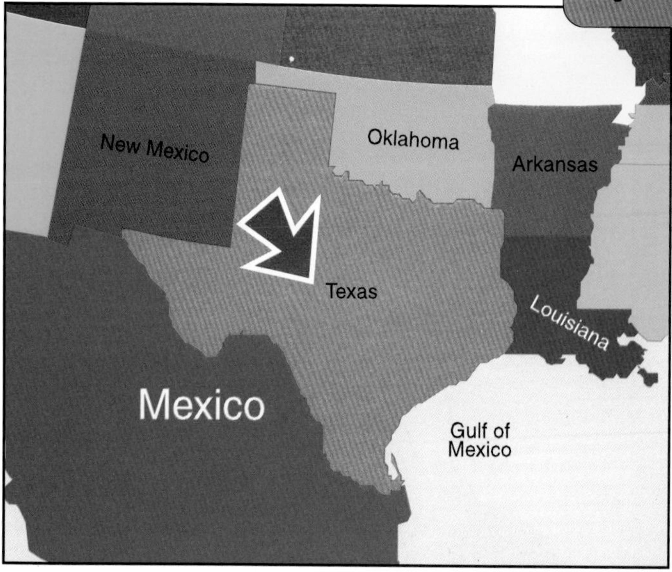

You Take the High Road!

Texas is 778 miles (1,252 kilometers) east to west... or west to east. Either way, it's a long drive!

Total Area: Approx. 267,277 square miles
Land Area: Approx. 261,914 square miles

Texas is 808 miles (1,300 kilometers) north to south... or south to north. Either way, it's still a long drive!

Texas was the largest state until Alaska joined the Union in 1959!
N
W
E
S

I'll Take the Low Road!

Highest Point

Guadalupe Peak — 8,749 feet above sea level (2,667 meters)

Guadalupe Peak in Culberson County is the highest point in Texas. The mountain lies within the Guadalupe Mountains National Park.

Lowest Point

Sea Level — Along Texas' extensive coastline at the Gulf of Mexico.

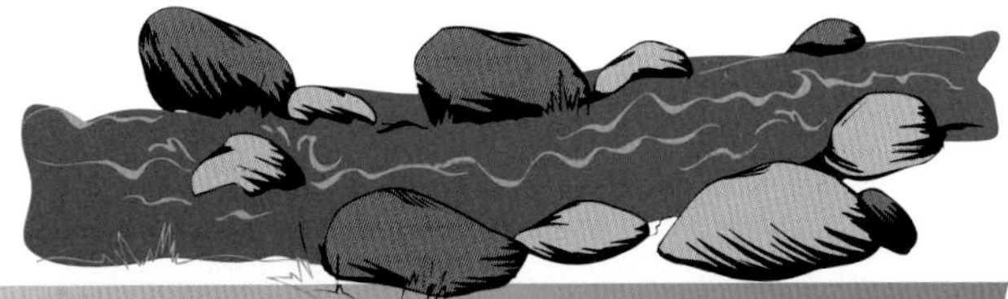

I'm Countying on You!

Texas is divided into 254 counties.

COUNTY: an administrative subdivision of a state or territory

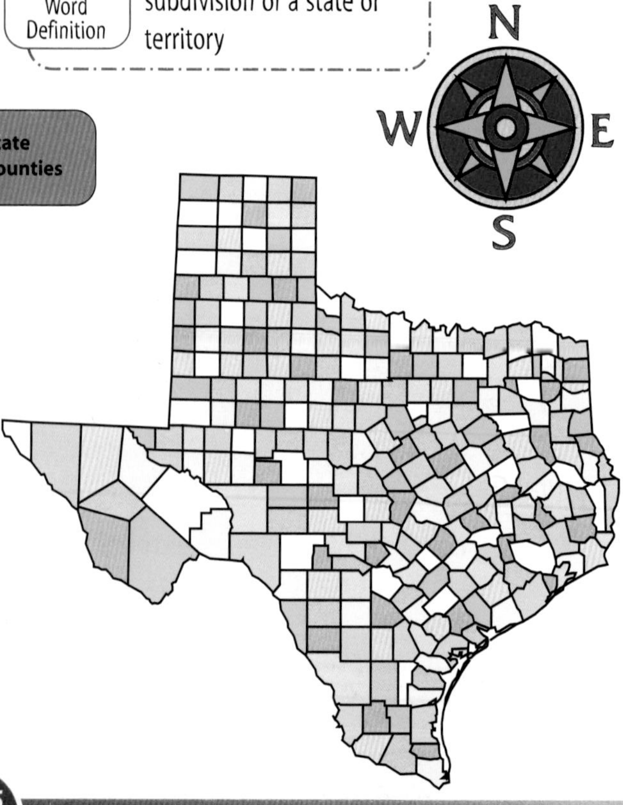

N
W
E
S

Natural Resources

Forests make up about 22 million acres of Texas land.

NATURAL RESOURCES: things that exist in or are formed by nature

Minerals:

- Oil
- Sulfur
- Helium
- Gypsum
- Clay
- Salt
- Natural Gas

Oil makes up more than 90% of mineral production in Texas. The first big oil strike in Texas occurred at Spindletop near Beaumont in 1901.

Deep-water ports like Houston allow large ships to deliver and export goods around the world.

Weather, Or Not?!

Texas' climate depends on which part of Texas you're in. Because Texas is such a large state, the weather on any day could be very different in a different part of the state.

Highest Temperature: 120°F (48.9°C) at Seymour on August 12, 1936

°F=Degrees Fahrenheit °C=Degrees Celsius

Lowest Temperature: -23°F (-30.6°C) at Seminole on February 8, 1933

The city of Amarillo in the Panhandle is likely to have snow every winter, but the average temperature in the lower Rio Grande Valley is 60°F (15.5°C).

BACK ON TOP

Texas' topography includes four land areas:

GULF COASTAL PLAINS

CENTRAL PLAINS

GREAT PLAINS

MOUNTAINS AND BASINS

Cap Rock Escarpment was formed by erosion. Geologists find this area very interesting because of the many ancient rocks and fossils poking up from the ground.

Word Definition

TOPOGRAPHY: the detailed mapping of the features of a small area or district

All of Texas' mountains are found west of the Pecos River, making this area popular with tourists.

Sea Level
100 m 328 ft
200 m 656 ft
500 m 1,640 ft
1,000 m 3,281 ft
2,000 m 6,562 ft
5,000 m 16,404 ft

King of the Hill

Mountains

El Capitan
Shumard Peak
Bartlett Peak
Bush Mountain
Hunter Peak

Ranges

Guadalupe
Hueco
Trans-Pecos
Chisos

Down the River

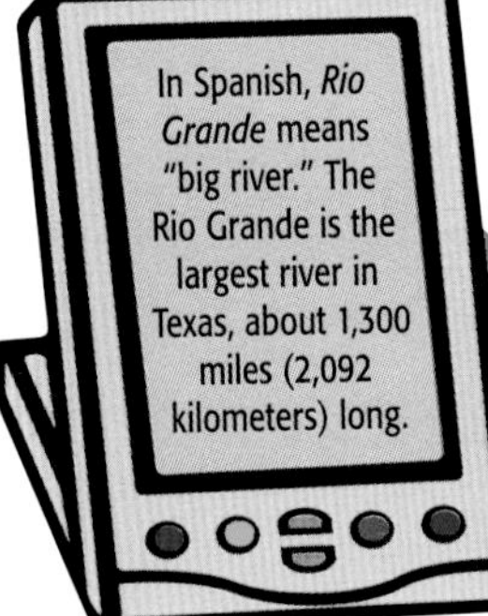

In Spanish, *Rio Grande* means "big river." The Rio Grande is the largest river in Texas, about 1,300 miles (2,092 kilometers) long.

Row, Row, Row your boat, gently down the stream…

- Sabine
- Red
- Rio Grande
- Pecos
- Brazos
- Canadian
- San Antonio
- Nueces
- Colorado
- Trinity
- Guadalupe

GONE FISHIN'

Major Lakes & Reservoirs

Sam Rayburn Reservoir in East Texas, which covers 113,400 acres, (45,927 hectares) is the largest body of water completely within Texas.

- Lake Texoma
- Lake Meredith
- Lake O' the Pines
- Lake Livingston
- Lake Buchanan
- Lake Travis
- Lake Austin
- Town Lake
- Amistad Reservoir
- Falcon Reservoir
- L.B. Johnson Reservoir

Word Definition

RESERVOIR: a body of water stored for public use

HOME TOWN

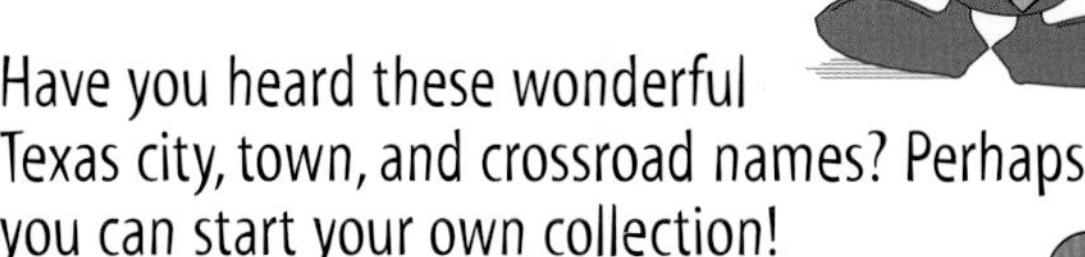

Have you heard these wonderful Texas city, town, and crossroad names? Perhaps you can start your own collection!

LARGER TOWNS:

Houston
San Antonio
Dallas
El Paso
Austin
Fort Worth
Arlington
Corpus Christi
Lubbock
Garland

SMALLER TOWNS:

Palestine
Claude
Boston
Robert Lee
Crane
Crosbyton
Paducah
San Diego
Clarendon
Eastland

Transportation

Major Interstate Highways

I-10, I-20, I-27, I-30, I-35
I-37, I-40 I-44, I-45

Texas roads cover more than 296,000 miles (476,366 kilometers).

Railroads

The railroad had an important role in the development of Texas. Texas has more railroad track than any other state 11,285 miles (18,161 kilometers).

Major Airports

Houston
Dallas-Fort Worth
San Antonio

Seaports

Houston
Galveston
Brownsville
Beaumont
Corpus Christi

Timeline

- 1519 Alonso Álvarez de Piñeda maps Texas coast
- 1528 Álvar Núñez Cabeza de Vaca explores Texas
- 1541 Coronado leads expedition across western Texas
- 1718 Mission San Antonio de Valero (the Alamo!) founded
- 1821 Stephen F. Austin begins to settle Texas
- 1836 Texas wins independence from Mexico
- 1839 Texas settlers defeat Cherokee near the Neches River
- 1845 Texas officially joins the Union as the 28th state
- 1848 Mexico surrenders claim to Texas
- 1861 Texas secedes from Union—joins Confederacy
- 1901 First big oil strike in Texas at Spindletop
- 1950 U.S. Supreme Court outlaws segregation
- 1953 Dwight D. Eisenhower becomes first Texas-born president
- 1963 President John F. Kennedy assassinated in Dallas—Vice-President Lyndon B. Johnson of Texas becomes president
- 1988 George Bush elected president
- 1999 Governor George W. Bush declares presidential candidacy
- 2001 Texas enters 21st century

Ney Cave was used as a base for Project X-ray during WWII. The project was a secret plan to drop thousands of bats, carrying firebombs, on Japan!

Here come the humans!

As early as 10,000 B.C. ancient peoples inhabited Texas. They may have originally come across a frozen bridge of land between Asia and today's Alaska. If so, they slowly traveled south and east until some settled in what would one day become the state of Texas.

These early people were nomadic hunters who traveled in small bands. They camped when seasons offered hunting, fishing, and fruit and nut gathering.

Native Americans Once Ruled!

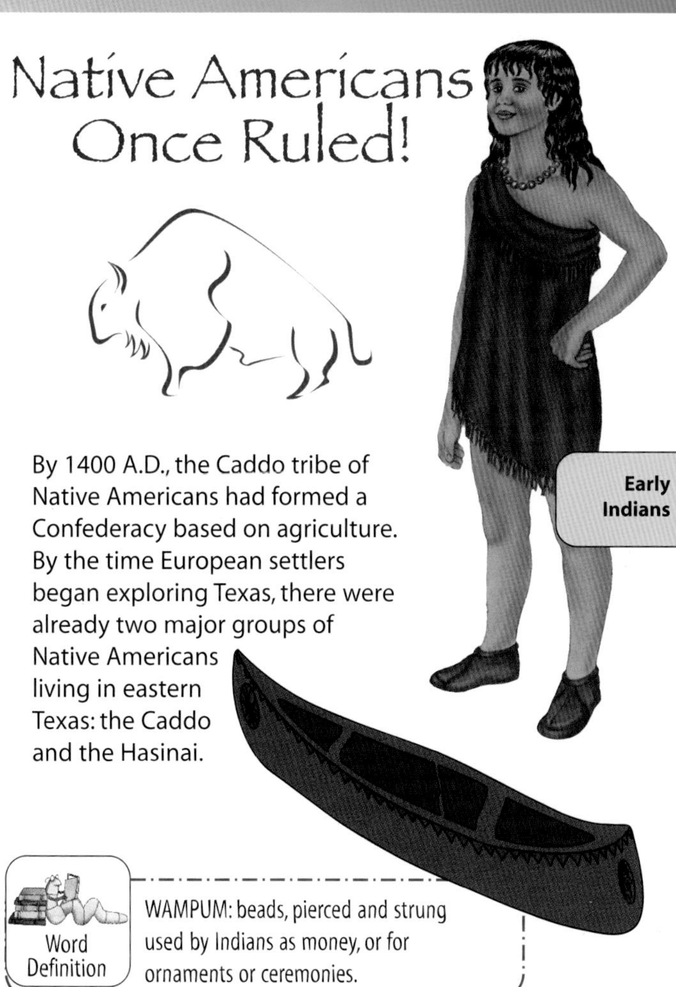

By 1400 A.D., the Caddo tribe of Native Americans had formed a Confederacy based on agriculture. By the time European settlers began exploring Texas, there were already two major groups of Native Americans living in eastern Texas: the Caddo and the Hasinai.

Word Definition

WAMPUM: beads, pierced and strung used by Indians as money, or for ornaments or ceremonies.

Land Ho!

The Spanish were the first Europeans to explore the state of Texas. They were lured here by stories of cities of gold and jewels. In 1540, Coronado led an expedition to discover the Seven Cities of Cibola and Quivira. The group wandered through Texas and East New Mexico, but they never found the mythical "cities of gold."

Early Explorers

Explorers,
missionaries,
and adventurers
came from
Europe on ships
in the 1500s.

Home, Sweet, Home

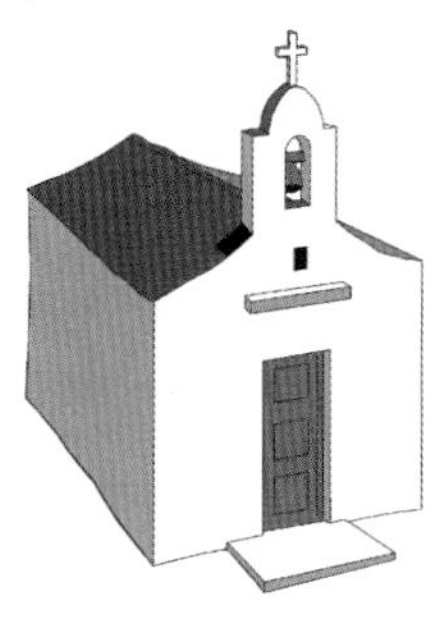

The first European settlement in Texas was a Spanish mission established in 1682 at Ysleta. The village was near the present day city of El Paso and was meant to bring Christianity to the native people. However, the missions were difficult to maintain and often abandoned. This made the Spanish claims to Texas land difficult to control. The land known as Texas now was fought over and colonized by the Spanish, French, and eventually Mexican and American settlers.

Magoffin Home State Historical Park–El Paso, Reconstruction of an 1875 adobe mansion containing many period furnishings and paintings.

Ysleta, considered one of the oldest towns in the state, became part of Texas when the Rio Grande changed its course.

Black Gold, Texas Tea

Oil makes up more than 90% of the state's mineral production. The discovery of large oil and natural gas deposits made many Texans rich. Millionaire Howard Hughes made his fortune by manufacturing drilling equipment, tank cars, and pipelines.

Native Americans used oil seeping from the ground for medicinal purposes. Survivors of the De Soto expedition used crude oil to caulk their boats!

Pecos Bill

Pecos Bill is a Texas legend. The story goes, he was lost as a baby, and raised by coyotes. When he grew up, he became an outlaw, an Indian fighter, and finally a cowboy. On a dare, he rode an Oklahoma Cyclone. Among his accomplishments, Pecos Bill wrestled bears and mountain lions, dug the Rio Grande, invented the six-gun and the lasso, taught cowboys to ride broncos, and fed his own horse barbed wire!

Of Human Bondage

Before Texas became a republic, the Mexican Government did not allow slavery. However, there is evidence that African–Americans have been in Texas as long as the first Spaniards. Immigrants from southern states brought their slaves with them in the 1820s, but the southern plantation system for raising crops hadn't reached farther than Eastern Texas when the Civil War began in 1861. Some people helped blacks escape slavery on the Underground Railroad, a route to the northern states where they could live free. Texans did not hear the Emancipation Proclamation until June 19, 1865 when the Union Army landed in Galveston. Have you ever heard of Juneteenth?

The Alamo

Texas fought for its independence from Mexico and became a republic. One of the most famous battles of the Texas Revolution was fought at the Alamo. For 13 days, 189 patriots held their own against 4,000 Mexican soldiers. Eventually the Mexicans killed everyone there except for a few women, children, and slaves. Texans got their revenge when a group of volunteers led by General Sam Houston defeated Santa Anna at San Jacinto. As they charged, the volunteers shouted, "Remember the Alamo!"

When Texas was still part of the Mexican Territory, Mexico revolted to win independence from Spain. Later, Texas fought for its independence from Mexico.

Brother

The Civil War was fought between the American states. The argument was over the right of the states to make their own decisions, including whether or not to own slaves. Some of the southern states began to secede (leave) the Union. They formed the Confederate States of America. In 1861, Texas joined this group. Richmond, Virginia was named the capital of the Confederacy.

Word Definition

RECONSTRUCTION: the recovery and rebuilding period following the Civil War.

The last battle of the Civil War was fought at Palmito Ranch, near Brownsville, on April 9, 1865 (more than a month after the Confederates had surrendered in Virginia!). Before computers, e-mail, fax, television, radio, and telephones, it was very difficult to send messages or communicate with people who were far away.

More Americans were killed during the Civil War than during World Wars I and II!

Get It In Writing!

Declaration of Independence, 1776, written by Thomas Jefferson

U.S. Constitution, 1787
The Constitution went into effect in 1789.

Texas Declaration of Independence, March 2, 1836

Treaty of Guadalupe Hidalgo, 1848, ended the Mexican War

Present Texas Constitution, adopted 1876

When the capital was moved from Austin to Houston in 1842, Austin citizens refused to give up government archives, which belonged in the capital city. The struggle became known as the Archives War. Austin eventually won this struggle and became Texas' capital permanently in 1872.

WELCOME TO AMERICA!

Texans have come to Texas from other states and many other countries on almost every continent! As time has gone by, Texas' population has grown more diverse. This means that people of different races and from different cultures and ethnic backgrounds have moved to Texas.

In the past, many immigrants came to Texas from Spain, Poland, Czechoslovakia, England, France, Germany, Scotland, Ireland, Serbia, Hungary, and other European countries. Slaves migrated (involuntarily) from Africa. More recently, people have migrated to Texas from South American and Asian countries. Only a certain number of immigrants are allowed to move to America each year. Many of these immigrants eventually become U.S. citizens.

1800s

Texas Fever or Texas Tick Fever was a major killer of cattle.

1900

Galveston hurricane and flood kills 8,000 people; worst natural disaster in U.S. history.

1947

Texas City explosion kills 408 people and injures 2,000.

1961

Hurricane Carla destroyed $300 million worth of property.

1993

Federal agents raid Branch Dividians near Waco; results in over 80 deaths.

Legal Stuff

Election-reform laws approved

1903

Child labor laws enacted

1906

State pure food and drug bill passed

1909

Bank-deposit insurance plan approved

Under the terms of its annexation agreement in 1849, Texas can subdivide into as many as five states! That would give Texans four more governors, eight more senators, and more votes in the Electoral College.

1901

Girls Industrial College established creating Texas' first women's college

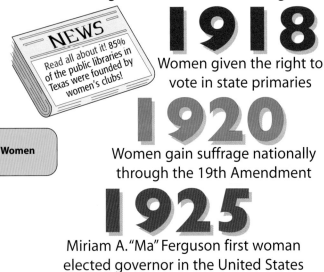

NEWS

Read all about it! 85% of the public libraries in Texas were founded by women's clubs!

1918

Women given the right to vote in state primaries

1920

Women gain suffrage nationally through the 19th Amendment

1925

Miriam A. "Ma" Ferguson first woman elected governor in the United States

1990

Ann Richards became the second woman elected governor of Texas

Word Definition

SUFFRAGE: the right or privilege of voting

Fight!, Fight!, Fight!

Wars that Texans participated in:

- **Mexican Revolution**
- **Texas Revolution**
- **Mexican War**
- **Civil War**
- **Indian Wars**
- **Spanish-American War**
- **World War I**
- **World War II**
- **Korean War**
- **Vietnam War**
- **Persian Gulf War**

During World War II, there were more than 70 prisoner-of-war camps in Texas, more than any other state. Most of them held German soldiers from the famed Afrika Korps; others held Italian and Japanese prisoners.

COWBOYS!

An authentic Texas cowboy would most likely wear a Stetson hat, a bandanna, maybe a homemade shirt, a vest to keep him warm, an oilcloth slicker in the rain, blue-jeans, chaps, and a pair of plain boots. High-heeled boots help keep cowboys' feet in the stirrups. Narrow toes make it easier to put feet through the stirrups. Texas cowboys usually wear spurs at all times.

Howdy partner!

Indian Tribes

- Caddo
- Arkokisa
- Attacapa
- Bidai
- Deadose
- Apache
- Comanche
- Kiowa

About 65,000 Native Americans live in Texas. Texas has three reservations: the Alabama-Coushatta Reservation; Ysleta del Sur Pueblo (Tigua Indian Reservation); and the Kickapoo Reservation.

Indian Tribes

Kickapoos enjoy special treatment from both the U.S. and Mexican governments. They can travel freely across the border between the two countries.

Quanah Parker was the son of a Comanche chief and a white settler. He became a chief and later took part in Theodore Roosevelt's inauguration.

Here, There, Everywhere!

ALONSO ÁLVAREZ DE PIÑEDA mapped the Texas Gulf Coast in 1519.

ÁLVAR NÚÑEZ CABEZA DE VACA wandered through Texas from 1528-1536. He and his fellow shipmates were held as slaves by Native Americans before finding Spanish settlements.

FRANCISCO VÁSQUEZ DE CORONADO searched for "cities of gold" through Texas in 1541. He didn't find them!

RENÉ-ROBERT CAVELIER, SIEUR DE LA SALLE built Fort St. Louis in 1685.

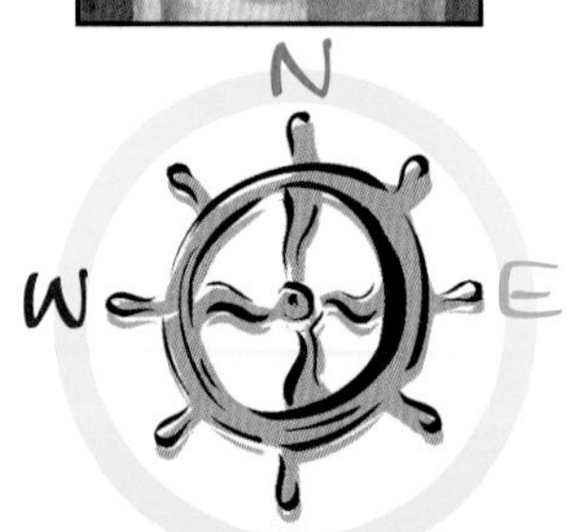

Founding Fathers

These Texans played especially important roles in Texas History!

STEPHEN F. AUSTIN—Father of Texas

SAM HOUSTON—President of the Republic of Texas, Governor of the State of Texas, U.S. Senator

MIRABEAU B. LAMAR—Father of Education, President of the Republic of Texas

Stephen F. Austin began to settle Texas while under contract with Mexico. Austin was an Empresario. In exchange for land, he brought families to settle Texas.

Founding Mothers

JANE LONG—Mother of Texas

THANKFUL "AUNT THANK" ALLIS—teacher for the Old Moulton Institute

ELIZABET NEY—sculptor, helped found the Texas Fine Arts Association

SARAH DODSON—created a lone star flag for her husband's militia company

ANNA SALAZAR DE ESPARZA—present at the Alamo with her husband, Gregorio Esparza, and children

MARÍA CORONEL (MOTHER MARÍA DE JESÚS)—"Woman in Blue;" the first bluebonnets were said to match the color of her cloak

Clara Driscoll and Adina De Zavala, along with the Daughters of the Republic of Texas, prevented the Alamo from being torn down to make way for a hotel in 1905. (You go, girls!)

Famous African-Americans

BILL PICKETT—cowboy, claimed to have invented steer wrestling

JOHN BIGGERS—painter and sculptor

HUDDIE LEDBETTER (LEADBELLY)—folk singer

JAMES FARMER—civil rights leader, founder of Congress of Racial Equality (CORE)

BARBARA JORDAN—first African–American elected to Texas Senate

BUFFALO SOLDIERS—After the Civil War, some of the African–American soldiers who remained in the Union Army helped in occupation forces. Because they admired their bravery, Native Americans named the soldiers after the animal they respected. All four regiments served at Fort McKavett.

Bandits and Rangers

Famous Texan Bandits and Lawmen!

Bank robber **Sam Bass** was gunned down by Texas Rangers in 1878.

Murderer **John Wesley Hardin** served a lengthy prison sentence for killing 31 people. He was shot to death shortly after his release in 1896.

Pancho Villa and his men crossed the Mexican border raiding Texas communities in 1916.

Texas Ranger **Frank Hamer** led a manhunt which ended the careers of **Bonnie Parker** and **Clyde Barrow** in a gunfight in 1934.

The **Newton Boys** became famous bank robbers and a movie was made about their escapades.

Check out the Texas Rangers hall of fame in Waco.

Famous Athletes

Jack Johnson—Heavyweight boxing champion

Nolan Ryan—Baseball player

Roger Staubach—Football player

"Slingin' Sammy" Baugh—Football player

Lance Armstrong—1st American cyclist on an American team to win the Tour de France

Mildred "Babe" Didrikson Zaharias—three time gold medalist in the 1932 Olympics. (She also set two world records!)

Willie Shoemaker—Jockey

Entertainers

★ SCOTT JOPLIN—Ragtime Music

★ BLIND LEMON JEFFERSON—Blues musician of the 1920s

★ FARRAH FAWCETT—Actress

★ ALBERT COLLINS—Texas bluesmar

★ BOB WILLS AND THE TEXAS PLAYBOYS—Pioneers of western swing

★ VAN CLIBURN—1958 International Tchaikovsky Piano Champion in Moscow

★ CAROL BURNETT—Actress, comedian

★ SELENA QUINTANILLA PEREZ—Singer

★ BUDDY HOLLY—Rock and roll pioneer

★ JANIS JOPLIN—Rock and roll singer, songwriter

★ GENE AUTRY—Singing cowboy

★ STEVIE RAY VAUGHN—Texas bluesman

★ ZZ TOP—Rock and roll band influenced by Texas blues

★ WILLIE NELSON—"Outlaw" country singer, songwriter

★ WAYLON JENNINGS—"Outlaw" country singer

★ TOMMY LEE JONES—Actor

★ GEORGE STRAIT—Country singer

The state musical instrument of Texas is the guitar.

PENS ARE MIGHTIER THAN SWORDS!

- ANDY ADAMS—known for *Log of a Cowboy*
- CARLOS E. CASTANEDA—wrote books on Texas and Mexican border history
- WILLIAM A. OWENS—wrote *This Stubborn Soil*
- DOBIE J. FRANK—educator, writer, folklorist, and Texas man of letters
- LARRY MCMURTRY—author *Lonesome Dove*
- KATHERINE ANNE PORTER—writer, 1966 Pulitzer Prize winner for her *Collected Stories*

The O. Henry Museum in Austin houses many of the short-story author's personal belongings and was his home while publishing the *Austin Weekly*, a short-lived newspaper.

E. Cormac McCarthy won the National Book Award for *All the Pretty Houses* in 1993.

nom de plume: French for *pen name*, a fictitious name under which a writer chooses to write

Lonesome Dove **was made into a popular movie series.**

DEEP IN THE ART OF TEXAS

Many Texas Artists have become famous for showing historical events, frontier scenes, and modern art. Do you know these Texas Artists?

- **Hermann Lungkwitz**
- **Richard Petri**
- **William Henry Huddle**
- **H.S. McArdle**

Luis Jimenez created a sculpture of a cowboy riding a bronco, which stands in Houston's Moody Park. **Elizabet Ney** came from Germany in1870 and became one of the state's most famous artists.

Neither **Charles M. Russell** nor **Frederick Remington** were from Texas, but they both glorified western life, such as the Texas Longhorn, cowboys, and Native Americans in their paintings, sculptures, and writings. You can see many of their works on display at the Sid Richardson Collection of Western Art at Sundance Square in Fort Worth.

Doctors

ASHBEL SMITH—Surgeon General of The Republic of Texas

FERID MURID—1998 Noble Prize in Medicine

DENTON COOLEY—Medical researcher and pioneer in open-heart surgery

MICHAEL E. DE BAKER—Surgeon, heart specialist, and medical researcher

One Texan, Dr. John R. Brinkley, sold "goat gland pills and elixir" in Del Rio. In 1933 he used his own radio station to sell his products.

Inventors

GAIL BORDEN, JR.—invented evaporated milk

JIM BOWIE—invented Bowie knife, popular knife used on the frontier

PERRY L. ADKISSON—1997 World Food Prize for developing an agriculture system which cuts the use of insecticides

Military Figures

JIM BOWIE—Commanded a group of volunteers at the Alamo; killed defending the Alamo

WILLIAM BARRET TRAVIS—Lieutenant colonel cavalry; killed defending the Alamo

SAM HOUSTON—General who led Texan Army to victory over Mexico

ADMIRAL CHESTER W. NIMITZ—Commander-in-chief of Pacific Fleet during World War II; has a class of aircraft carriers named for him

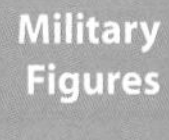

DWIGHT DAVID EISENHOWER—Attained rank of five-star general during WWII; Born in Dennison

AUDIE MURPHY—Most decorated American soldier of WWII

DAVID CROCKETT—Led group of volunteers in the Texas Revolution; killed defending the Alamo

Political Leaders

- Sam Rayburn—Speaker of the U.S. House of Representatives longer than anyone else, a total of seventeen years

- John Nance "Cactus Jack" Garner—vice president of the U.S. from 1933-1941

- Martin Dies, Jr.—First Chairman House Committee on Un-American Activities

- Henry G. Cisneros, Mayor of San Antonio—1982-1990; U.S. cabinet member

- Dwight D. Eisenhower—34th U.S. president, born in Denison; established interstate highway system

- Lyndon B. Johnson—36th U.S. president, struggled for Civil Rights Act of 1964

- George Bush—41st U.S. president, saw the Soviet Union collapse, and the fall of the Berlin Wall

- J. Pinckney Henderson was the state's first governor.
- Sam Houston served as President of the Republic of Texas, but also served as governor.
- James S. Hogg was Texas' first native-born governor.
- Miriam A. Ferguson was Texas' first woman governor.
- Ann Richards was Texas' second woman governor.
- George W. Bush announced his campaign for U.S. presidency in 1999.

The Jim Hogg State Historical Park preserves the birthplace of Texas' first native-born governor.

JURISTS

- Tom C. Clark—U.S. Attorney General and U.S. Supreme Court Justice
- Sandra Day O'Connor—First woman to serve as U.S. Supreme Court Justice
- James S. Hogg—Governor, State Attorney General
- Roy Bean—Frontier Justice of the Peace dealt frontier justice from his saloon!

Keeping the Faith

Here are some of Texas' most revered places of worship:

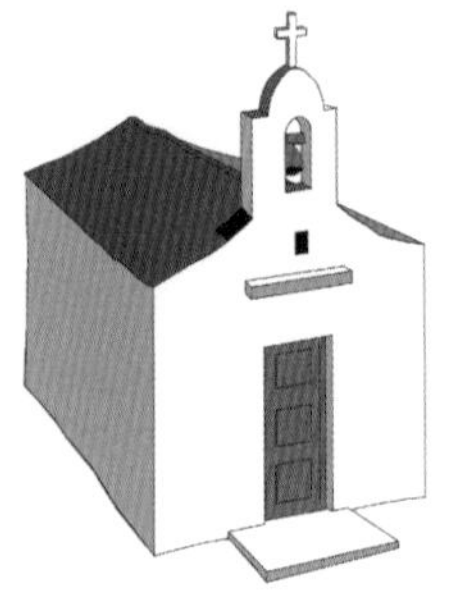

Guadalupe Mission
Mission Concepcion
Mission Espada
Mission Espiritu Santo
Mission San Antonio de Valero (Alamo)
Mission San Jose (Queen of the Missions)
Mission San Juan
Mission Senora de los Ais (Dolores Mission)
Oblate Mission
Rothko Chapel
San Augustin de la Isleta del Sur
San Fernanado Cathedral in San Antonio
Socorro Mission
Ysleta Mission

Goliad State Historical Park is home to the longest running mission in Texas, over 100 years.

SCHOOLS

Colleges and Universities in Texas:

Austin College, Sherman (1849)
Saint Mary's University of San Antonio (1852)
Trinity University, San Antonio (1869)
Texas Christian University (1873)
Texas A & M University, College Station (1876)
Sam Houston State University, Huntsville (1879)
University of Texas at Austin (1883)
Rice University, Houston (1891)
Our Lady of the Lake University of San Antonio (1895)
Southwest Texas State University, San Marcos (1903)
Texas Tech University, Lubbock (1923)

In 1840, Southwestern University in Georgetown became the first institution of higher learning in Texas. In 1845, the year Texas became a state, Baylor University was founded.

Historic Sites and Parks

Historic Sites

Fort Davis National Historic Site
Caddoan Mounds State Historical Park
Fort Griffin State Historical Park
Fort Lancaster State Historical Park
Hueco Tanks State Historical Park
Mission Tejas State Historical Park
Monument Hill State Historic Site
San Antonio Missions National Historic Park
San Jacinto Battleground State Historical Park
Texas State Railroad Historical Park

National Parks

★ Big Bend National Park consists of mountains, desert, and unusual geological forms located within the large bend of the Rio Grande.
★ Guadalupe Mountains National Park encompasses an extensive fossil reef, a tremendous earth fault, and unusual plants and animals.

State Parks

Abilene
Bentsen-Rio Grande Valley
Blanco
Brazos Bend
Caddo Lake
Caprock Canyons
Davis Mountains
Dinosaur Valley
Falcon
Galveston Island
Goose Island
Mustang Island
Palmetto
Possum Kingdom

Early Residency

★ Cabin of John Neely Bryan—1841 home belonged to the founder of the city of Dallas

★ Greek Revival Governors Mansion—1885 home; oldest public building in Austin

★ Berkeley Plantation—Charles City

★ Bishop's Palace—Named for the bishop of Galveston who moved into the home in 1923.

★ Jose Antonio Navarro House—San Antonio, home of Texan who signed the Texas Declaration of Independence.

★ Spanish Governor's Palace—San Antonio, 1749 home once housed Spanish officials when Texas was still ruled by Spain.

★ Laguna Gloria—now houses the Austin Museum of Art. The mansion was once the home of Clara Driscol, "Savior of the Alamo."

A few of Texas' famous Battlefields

- San Jacinto Battleground State Historical Park—commemorates Texas' independence from Mexico.
- Fannin Battleground—site of famous Texas Revolution Battle.
- Lipantitlan—near the sites of an 1835 battle during the Texas Revolution and a Mexican fort of the same name.
- Sabine Pass Battleground—site of 1863 Civil War battle that saved Texas.

- Palmito Hill Battlefield—site of the last battle of the Civil War.

Battleship Texas State Historic Site–The *USS Texas* in Houston, a restored dreadnought, is the oldest surviving naval vessel veteran of both World Wars! *USS Texas* was designated the state ship in 1995.

In 1858, the Army imported camels for use in the deserts of western Texas.

Libraries

- GEORGE BUSH LIBRARY, College Station
- LYNDON BAINES JOHNSON PRESIDENTIAL LIBRARY AND MUSEUM, Austin
- AMARILLO PUBLIC LIBRARY, Amarillo
- AMON CARTER MUSEUM PHOTOGRAPHIC ARCHIVES, Fort Worth

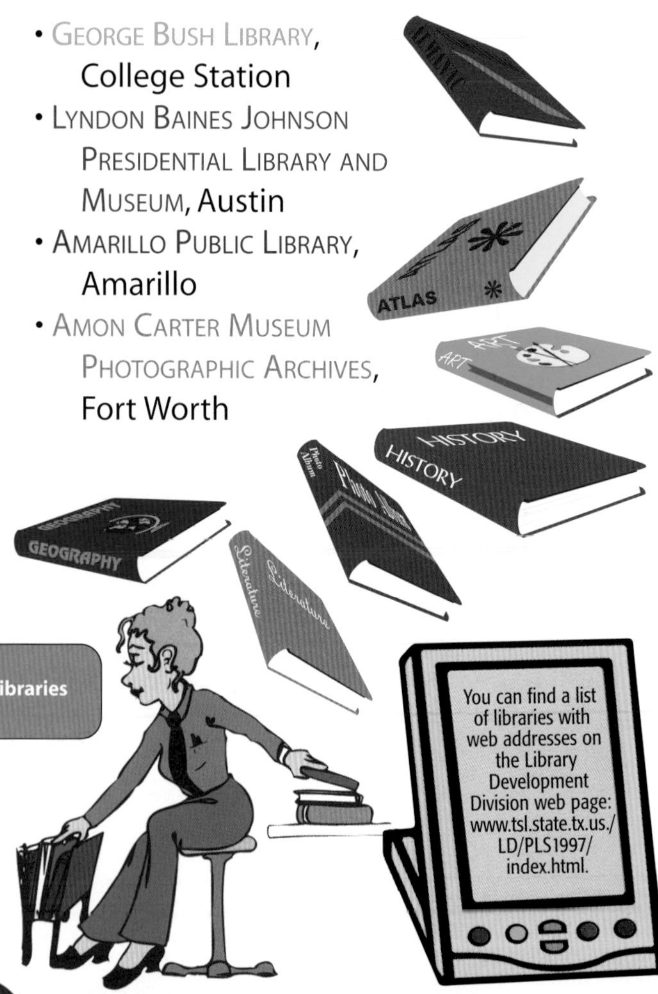

You can find a list of libraries with web addresses on the Library Development Division web page: www.tsl.state.tx.us./LD/PLS1997/index.html.

Dallas Zoo

Fort Worth Zoo

Gladys Porter Zoo, Brownsville

Houston Zoological Gardens

San Antonio Zoo

Texas Zoo, Victoria

Texas State Aquarium, Corpus Christi

Matagorda Island State Park and Wildlife Management Area

Museums

- Texas has over 700 local history museums. A few include:
- Kimbell, Fort Worth
- Amon Carter, Fort Worth
- Modern Art Museum, Fort Worth
- Stockyards Museum, and Cattleman's Museum, Fort Worth.
- Sixth Floor Museum, Dallas (Preserves the spot where Lee Harvey Oswald shot President John F. Kennedy)
- Texas Memorial Museum, Austin
- Panhandle Plains Historical Museum, Canyon
- Old West Museum, Sunset
- Native–American Cultural Heritage Museum, Dallas
- Tigua Pueblo Museum, El Paso
- Ysleta Del Sur Pueblo Museum, El Paso

MONUMENTS

- Alibates Flint Quarries, Early Native Americans dug here for limestone to make arrowheads, knives, and other tools. This is Texas' only national monument.
- Monument Hill State Historic Site
- John F. Kennedy Memorial, Dallas
- Alamo, San Antonio
- San Jacinto Monument, near Houston

SPACE PLACE!

The Lyndon B. Johnson Space Center is located in Houston. There, you can see moon rocks, the Skylab Trainer, and actual space vehicles from the 1960s Project Mercury to the present day space shuttles.

The Arts

THE INSTITUTE OF TEXAN CULTURES in San Antonio is home to exhibits of more than 27 ethnic groups who have contributed their cultures to the state of Texas, including Native Americans, Spanish, and Dutch.

THE MENIL COLLECTION is housed in a specially designed building in Houston. Everything from Medieval and Byzantine art to contemporary and surrealist art exhibits are on display.

Sul Ross State University has an annual COWBOY POETRY GATHERING in February.

THE AZTEC THEATER in San Antonio is famous for its Aztec and Mayan influenced architecture.

Cowboys learn to rope
and ride.
They wear their boots
and spurs.
They'll wear a lasso by
their side,
and rustle up the
restless herd.
–Chad,
a cowboy poet

Seashores and Lighthouses

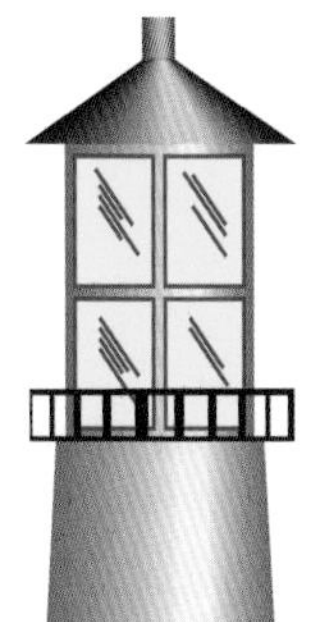

Texas has one National Seashore, called **PADRE ISLAND**. The Padre Island National Seashore has about 67 miles (108 kilometers) of beautiful white sand beaches.

Texas has had many lighthouses. Some are still in use today, while others have become too old to remain in use. The Brazos Santiago light is still active near the Mexican border.

ROADS

After the Civil War, THE CHISOLM TRAIL played an important role in the development of Austin and the cattle industry. Highway 81 follows the route of the old Chisolm Trail from Fort Worth to Newton, Kansas.

EL CAMINO REAL or "The Royal Highway," also known as the OLD SAN ANTONIO ROAD, linked colonial Mexico with Spanish settlements in Texas and Louisiana. It originally followed Native–American trails and was eventually incorporated into the state highway system in 1929 as Highway 21.

CHANNEL

Although 50 miles (80 kilometers) inland, Houston is Texas' largest port! A large ship channel built in 1914 connects the city with Galveston Bay. Channelview City has a terrific view of the channel.

Caves and Caverns

CAVES

Hey Spelunkers! Check out "down under" Texas!

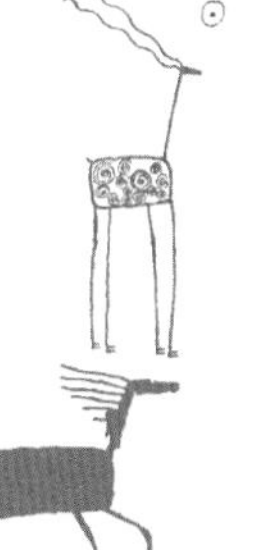

- Bracken Cave (Bat Colony)
- Carlsbad Caverns
- Cascade Caverns
- Cave Without a Name
- Caverns of Sonora
- Inner Space Cavern
- Longhorn Cavern State Park
- Natural Bridge Caverns

Seminole Canyon State Park has many cave paintings called pictographs.

A *spelunker* is a person who goes exploring caves!

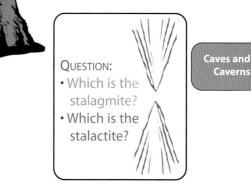

Question:
- Which is the stalagmite?
- Which is the stalactite?

Answer: Stalactites are long, tapering formations hanging from the roof of a cavern, produced by continuous watery deposits containing certain minerals. The mineral-rich water dripping from stalactites often forms conical stalagmites on the floor below.

Animals of Texas

Texas animals include:

White-tailed Deer
Black Bear
Bobcat
Opossum
Raccoon
Elk
Desert cottontail
Black-tailed jackrabbit
Prairie dog
Pronghorn
Armadillo
Badger
Striped skunk
Mountain lion
Fox
Coyote
Mountain Sheep

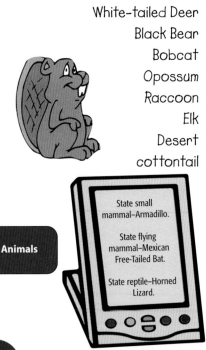

State small mammal–Armadillo.
State flying mammal–Mexican Free-Tailed Bat.
State reptile–Horned Lizard.

Texas Endangered Species

Some endangered animal species found in Texas:

Ocelot

Red Wolf

Greater long-nosed bat

Black-footed ferret

Jaguarundi

Texas blind salamander

Houston toad

Riddle:

What do you get when you cross a Greater long-nosed bat with a Texas blind salamander?

Answer: A long-nosed salamander or a Texas blind bat!

To find out more about Texas' endangered and threatened species, go to the Texas Parks and Wildlife Departments web page at: www.tpwd.state.tx.us/nature/endang/endang.htm
Wooow! This is so exciting!

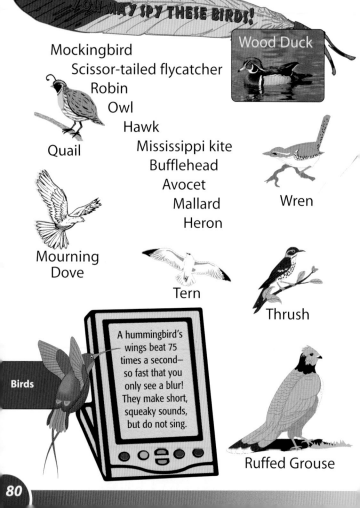

You may spy these birds!

Wood Duck

Mockingbird
Scissor-tailed flycatcher
Robin
Owl
Hawk
Mississippi kite
Bufflehead
Avocet
Mallard
Heron

Quail

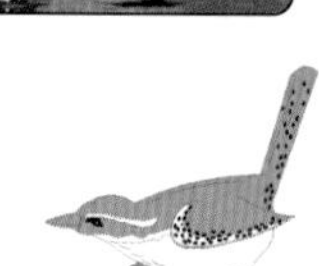
Wren

Mourning Dove

Tern

Thrush

A hummingbird's wings beat 75 times a second—so fast that you only see a blur! They make short, squeaky sounds, but do not sing.

Ruffed Grouse

Don't let these Texas bugs bug you!

Dragonfly
Damselfly
Katydid
Stick insect
Termite
Giant water bug
Water strider
Assassin bug
Periodical cicada
Spittlebug
Ant lion
Longhorn beetle
Weevil

Bumblebee

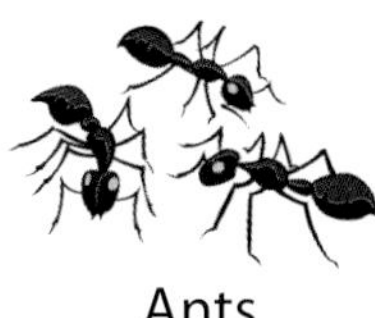

Ants

Butterfly

Praying Mantis

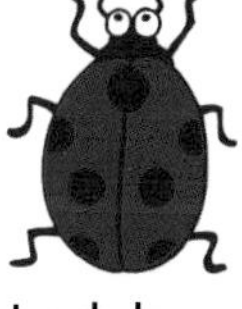

Ladybug

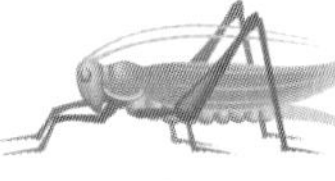

Grasshopper

Do we know any of these bugs?
Maybe... Hey, that ladybug is cute!

Whirligig Beetles have two pairs of eyes – one pair looks above the water, the other looks under it!

Fish

Swimming in Texas waters:

Catfish
Sunfish
Paddle Fish
Striped Bass
Crappie
Bluegill
Walleye
Northern Pike
Trout
Largemouth Bass
Smallmouth Bass

Sea Critters

In Texas' seas,
you may find:
Croaker
Black Drum
Grouper
Mackerel
Red Drum
Red Snapper
Sheepshead
Flounder
Seatrout
Tarpon
Tuna
Barracuda
Giant Squid
Bottlenose dolphins send messages to each other by whistling and squealing. They will help an injured dolphin get to the surface so it can breathe!

Seashells

She sells Seashells by the Texas Seashore!

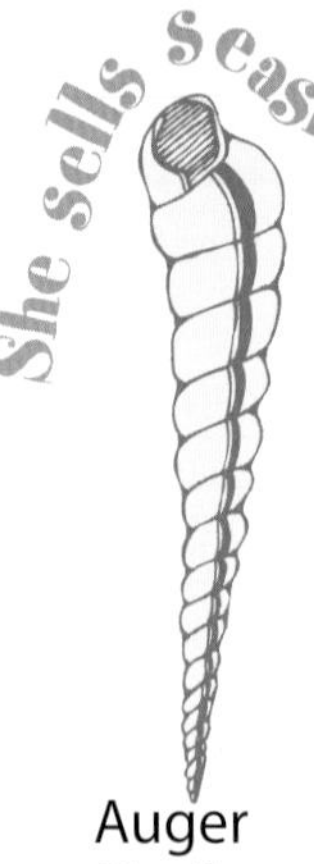

Auger Shell

chiton
cerith
conch
slipper shell
worm shell
cowrie
helmet shell
wentletrap
janthina
whelk
murex
cone shell
vampire shell
sundial shell
bubble shell
tusk shell
oyster
scallop
cockle
angel wing
shipworm

Lightning Whelk

Olive Shell

Periwinkle

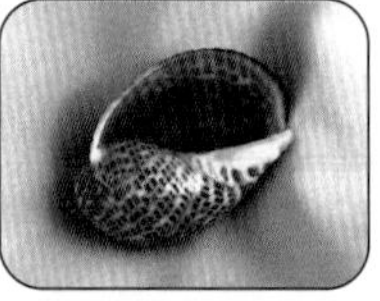

The Lightning Whelk, found only on the Gulf Coast, is Texas' state shell.

Moon Shell

Coquina

TREEMENDOUS!

THESE TREES TOWER OVER TEXAS:

Loblolly pine
Shortleaf pine
Sweetgum
Hickory
Elm
Mesquite
Pecan
Osage

Texas has four national forests: Angelina, Davy Crockett, Sabine, and Sam Houston.

Are you crazy about these Texas wildflowers?
Prickly pear
Bluebonnet
Indian paintbrush
Firewheel
Chicory
Oxeye daisy
Lupine
Blazing star
Globemallow
Seashore mallow
Cardinal flower
Greasewood
Bear grass
The cat claw acacia, or "wait-a-minute bush" gets its nickname from hikers who get stuck in the plants thorny clutches and must shout, "Wait a minute!"

Cream of the Crops

Texas' principal agricultural products:

The lower Rio Grande River Valley has an eleven-month growing season which makes for a lot of winter vegetables and citrus fruits.

The **first rodeo** ever was held in Pecos, Texas in 1883.

Wiley Post, born near Grand Plain, Texas became the **first person to fly solo around the world** in 1933.

The **first Rattlesnake Derby** was held in McCamey, Texas in 1936; $200 went to the winner.

Biggest attended event in the country, Texas State Fair held in Dallas at Fair Park.

San Jacinto Monument is the **tallest monument in the U.S.** It marks the site of the battle which won Texas' independence from Mexico.

Rusk, Texas has the **world's longest foot bridge**; 547 feet (168 meters).

The **smallest state park in the U.S.** is Acton State Historical Park, near Granbury, burial site of Davy Crockett's second wife, Elizabeth Patton.

Festivals

GREAT WATERMELON THUMP—Luling; They have a watermelon seed spitting contest, too!

WORLD'S CHAMPION CHILI COOK-OFF—Terlingua

Fiesta—San Antonio

RATTLESNAKE ROUNDUP—Sweetwater

TEXAS FOLKLIFE FESTIVAL—University of Texas Institute of Texan Cultures at San Antonio.

Carnival Season—Mardi Gras is celebrated in many Gulf Coast communities.

Important Dates

New Year's Day, *January 1*

Sam Rayburn Day, *January 6*

Martin Luther King Day, *3rd Monday of January*

Presidents' Day, *3rd Monday of February*

Texas Independence Day, Texas Flag Day, Sam Houston Day , *March 2*

Cinco de Mayo, *May 5*

Memorial Day, *last Monday in May*

Emancipation Day in Texas (Juneteenth), *June 19*

Independence Day, *July 4*

Columbus Day *2nd Monday in October*

Father of Texas (Stephen F. Austin) Day, *November 3*

Thanksgiving Day, *4th Thursday in November*

Famous Food

Texas is famous for the following delicious foods!

Tacos
Tortillas
Chicken Fried Steak
Picante sauce
Cabrito
Kolaches
Barbecue
Menudo
Guacamole
Enchiladas
Fajitas
Barbecue
Chili
Tex-Mex

State native pepper–Chiltepin
State pepper–Jalapeño
State vegetable–Sweet Texas Onion
State fruit–Texas Red Grapefruit
State dish–Chili

Takin' Care of Business

Oil, petrochemicals, agriculture, banking, insurance, railroad, and military bases are all important businesses and trades in Texas. Famous Texas companies include Texaco, Imperial Holly Corporation, Sealy Mattress Company, El Fenix, Texas Instruments, and Blockbuster. In recent years, Texas has become an important center for the computer, aviation, and space industries.

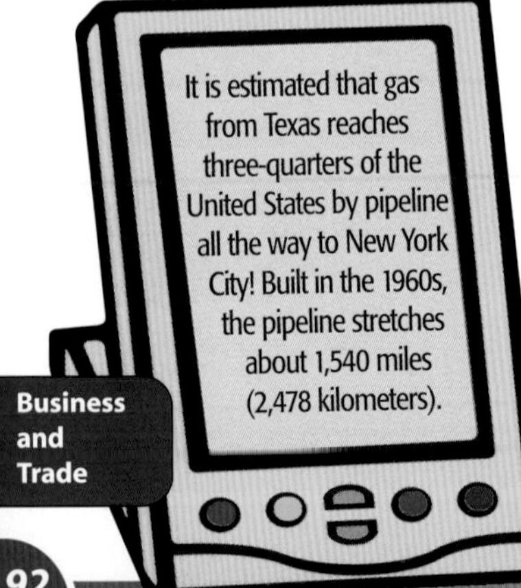

It is estimated that gas from Texas reaches three-quarters of the United States by pipeline all the way to New York City! Built in the 1960s, the pipeline stretches about 1,540 miles (2,478 kilometers).

Books & Websites

America the Beautiful Texas, Conrad Stein
Let's Discover the States: The Southwest, Chelsea House
My First Book About Texas, Carole Marsh
Portrait of America: Texas, Kathleen Thompson
Texas Folklife Festival: A Childrens Guide, Kathy Wicks
Texas Jeopardy, Carole Marsh
Texas Jography: A Fun Run Through Our State, Carole Marsh

COOL TEXAS WEBSITES
www.state.tx.us
www.governor.state.tx.us
www.thc.state.tx.us
www.sos.state.tx.us
www.ci.farmers-branch.tx.us
www.texasalmanac.com
www.austintexas.org
www.traveltex.com
www.texasexperience.com
www.gallopade.com

Texas Glossary

GLOSSARY WORDS

conjunto - A special type of Texas-Mexican music which combines traditional Mexican music with polka tunes borrowed from the Germans and Czechs.

hacendado - A ranch owner

immigrant - A person who moves from one country to a new one, then settles permanently in the new country.

mestizos - people of mixed Spanish and Native-American Heritage.

panhandle - A long or narrow strip of land stretching out from a larger territory.

revolution - A complete overthrow of an existing government, usually by force.

vaquero - Early Spanish cowboy

wildcatter - An oil explorer who is willing to drill for oil in places it has never been found before.

Texas Spelling Bee

Here are some special Texas-related words to learn! To take the Spelling Bee, have someone call out the words and you spell them aloud or write them on a piece of paper.

Spelling Words

aqueduct	governor
armadillo	Guadalupe
bluebonnet	mockingbird
cantaloupe	monarch
capital	mission
capitol	petroleum
climate	Ranger
empresario	Rio Grande
enchiladas	reservoir
geology	topography

ABOUT THE AUTHOR...

CAROLE MARSH has been writing about Texas for more than 20 years. She is the author of the popular Texas State Stuff series for young readers and creator, along with her son, Michael Marsh, of "Texas Facts and Factivities," a CD-ROM widely used in Texas schools. The author of more than 100 Texas books and other supplementary educational materials on the state, Marsh is currently working on a new collection of Texas materials for young people. Marsh correlates her Texas materials to Texas' Essential Knowledge and Skills for Social Studies. Many of her books and other materials have been inspired by or requested by Texas teachers and librarians.

Exemplary Editorial Assistant:
Chad Beard